I0108317

# Beautiful Sister

## Beth P. Bolden

Be Bold About It, LLC
Atlanta, Georgia

**Beautiful Sister**

Copyright © 2021 by Beth P. Bolden
All rights reserved.

No part of this book can be produced in whole or in part, or stored in a retrieval system, or transmitted in any form or by any means, without permission of the publisher.

Special Thanks to Ignastius Reeves for your creative editing.

Scripture quotation marked (AMP) is taken from the *Amplified® Bible*.
Copyright © 2015 by The Lockman Foundation. Used by permission. www.Lockman.org

Scripture quotation marked (NLT) is taken from the *Holy Bible, New Living Translation*.
Copyright © 1996, 2004, 2007 by Tyndale House Foundation. Used by permission of Tyndale House Publishers, Inc., Carol Stream, IL 60188. All rights reserved.

Scripture quotation marked (MSG) is taken from *The Message*. Copyright © 1993, 1994, 1995, 1996, 2000, 2001, 2002. Used by permission of NavPress Publishing Group.

Illustrated by Sonny Heston
All rights reserved.

ISBN: 978-1-7325964-1-2

For bulk purchases and discounts for nonprofit organizations, contact bethpbolden@gmail.com

Connect with Beth P. Bolden!

f @skincolorbeauty

@skincolorbeauty

@imboldinmyblack

This book is dedicated to my brother, Brian Leon Bolden whom I have observed from childhood treat women and girls with the utmost respect, starting with our mother, Marynette Reid Bolden, me, your wife Roni, and your daughter, Briana, our aunts, cousins, my friends and your students.  You are a male example and role model that the world needs to see and emulate.

To all the women and girls who will read this book, Your self-image is defined by a loving God that formed you to be fearfully and wonderfully made. You are one of a kind and so special. Live your life with purpose being better than you were the day before.  You will always win because you are your only comparison. You are the prize!

Beautiful sister, that's me! I am created in the image of someone very special.

He is so special; He adorned me with beauty throughout all of me.  He adorned me with gifts he allows me to share.  These gifts are ones that I can take with me everywhere.

"God created human beings; he created them God like, reflecting God's nature." —Genesis 1:27 (MSG)

As I display these gifts others can easily tell, that beauty is not only outside of me, but on the inside as well.  Sometimes when people first meet me they say, "You're so pretty" or "She's so cute." But when they really get to know me they see my spiritual fruit.

"But the fruit of the Spirit is love, joy, peace, patience, kindness, goodness, faithfulness, gentleness, and self-control."
—Galatians 5:22-23 (AMP)

It doesn't matter the color of my skin, the length or texture of my hair, the color of my eyes, or the brand of clothes I wear. It's not my heritage, my culture or the country I'm from.

It's not earrings in my ears, rings on my fingers, watches around my wrists or bracelets climbing my arm.

"Your beauty should not come from outward adornment, such as elaborate hairstyles and the wearing of gold jewelry or fine clothes. Rather, it should be that of your inner self, the unfading beauty of a gentle and quiet spirit, which is of great worth in God's sight."
—I Peter 3:3-4 (AMP)

My beauty is based neither upon where I live, where I go to school, nor who my parents are or who they are not. It's not my talents or skills; it's not even the church I attend.

It's not the car I ride in or how much money I have to spend because on that, my beauty does not depend.

What is it that makes me beautiful?

# It is …

I accepted Jesus Christ as my Lord and Savior,
On the cross He sacrificed. Yet, in my heart is
where He lives and his love in me shines bright!
Jesus is everything to me; the one that I pray to.
He guides, comforts, and protects me and He'll
do the same for you. Because of all these things,
I'm beautiful in my heart. When God begins to
look for beauty that's the first place He starts.

"For God loved the world so much that he gave his one and only son,
so that everyone who believes in him will not perish but have eternal
life." —John 3:16 (NLT)

All my beauty cannot be seen with just an outward view. When you accept Christ in your life your beauty will shine through. This beauty I have is not mine alone; it was given to me to share.  And if you accept Jesus Christ as your Lord, you'll have your own fruit you can bear. You can begin bearing fruit starting today by saying the words of this prayer and believing these words with all your heart:

*Father, I confess that I am a sinner.  I believe that Jesus Christ died for my sins on the cross and was raised from the dead for my justification.  I do now receive and confess Him as my personal Savior.*

And with this prayer you can receive the gift of God's grace and a rebirth; along with the promise of a life spent in heaven after your life here on Earth.  If you have prayed this prayer with a sincere heart you are now a child of God. A child who is beautiful inside and out.

What makes you beautiful?
Write down ten things that reflect how God "fearfully and wonderfully" created you.

_____

_____

_____

_____

_____

_____

_____

_____

_____

_____

_____

_____

_____

_____

_____

_____

_____

_____

_____

_____

Do you have a sister? If not, who is "like a sister" to you?
Write down ten things that reflect how God "fearfully and
wonderfully" created her.

_____

_____

_____

_____

_____

_____

_____

_____

_____

_____

_____

_____

_____

_____

_____

_____

_____

_____

_____

_____

_____

_____

# Other Books by Beth P. Bolden

## *There's Nothing Wrong with the Color of My Skin*

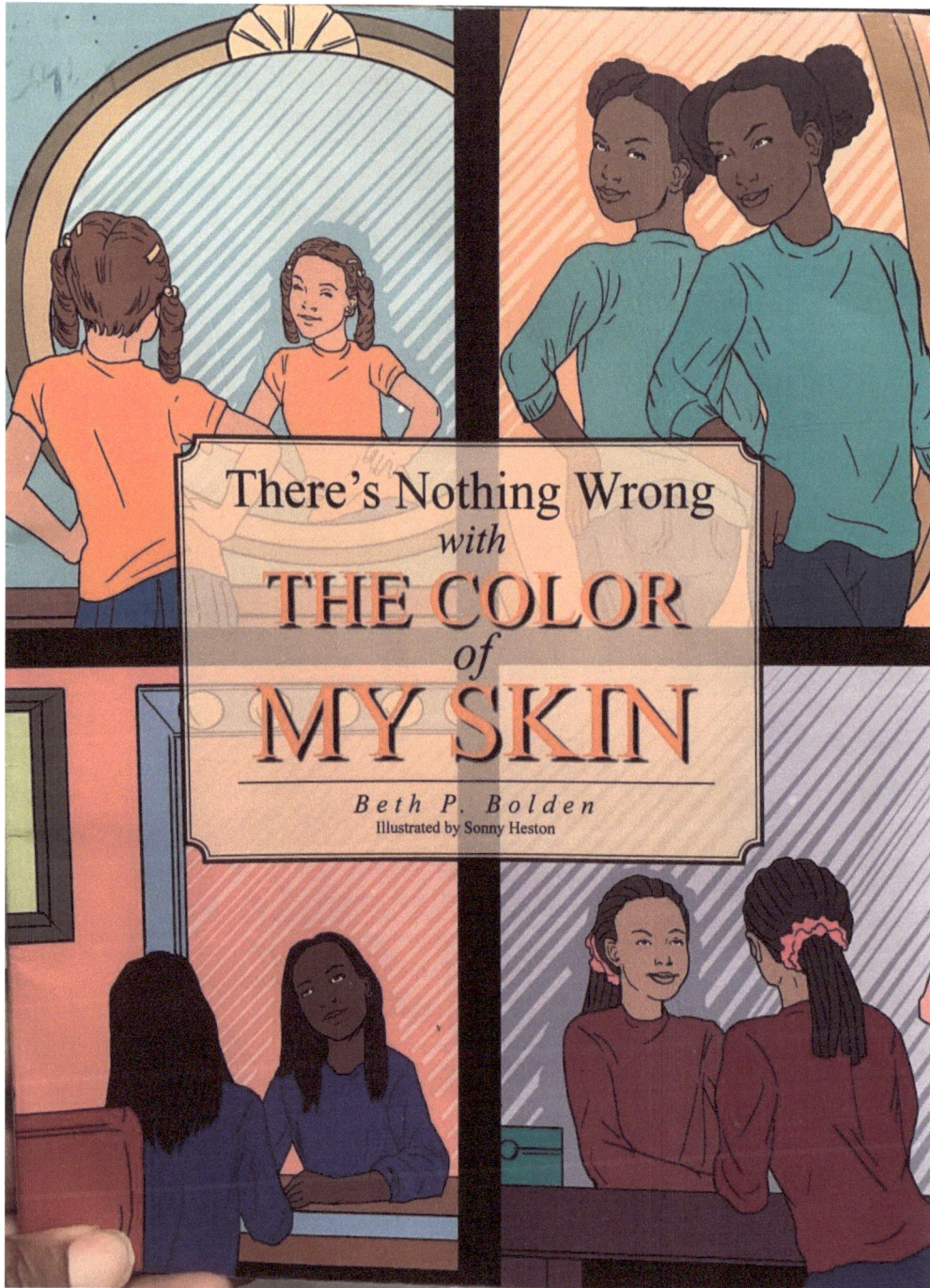

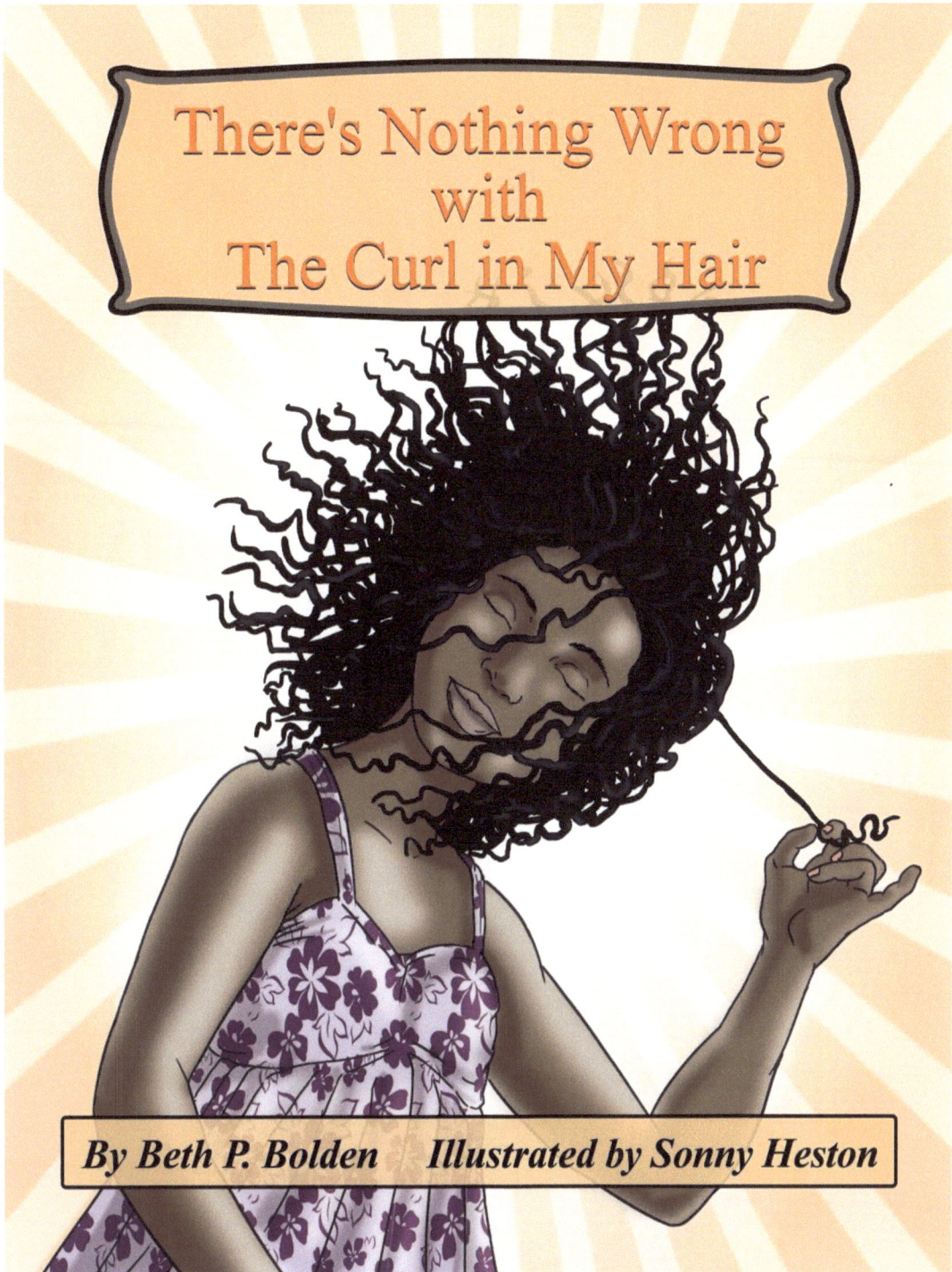

There's Nothing Wrong
with
The Curl in My Hair

By Beth P. Bolden    Illustrated by Sonny Heston

Beth P. Bolden's books are available at the following fine bookstores:

**Avant-garde Books, LLC**
www.avantgardebooks.net

**Nubian Bookstore**
1540 Southlake Parkway, Suite 7A
Atlanta, Georgia 30260

**The Listening Tree**
www.listeningtreebooks.com

www.ingramcontent.com/pod-product-compliance
Lightning Source LLC
Chambersburg PA
CBHW041558040426
42447CB00002B/225

* 9 7 8 1 7 3 2 5 9 6 4 1 2 *